So you're
only human

So you're only human

LILY M. GYLDENVAND

Augsburg Publishing House
Minneapolis, Minnesota

SO YOU'RE ONLY HUMAN
© Augsburg Publishing House 1957
Library of Congress Catalog Card No. 57-14795

Manufactured in the United States of America

Who knows how many miracles
have never happened because someone
quit trying and took refuge in the
excuse: "After all, I'm only human!"

FOREWORD

"After all, I'm only human!"

Thus we console ourselves when we can't cope with life situations. We concentrate so intently upon our limitations that we don't see our tremendous possibilities. We are so concerned with apologizing for our inadequacies that we forget that God's Word says:

"I can do all things through Christ who strengthens me . . ."

"My God shall supply every need of yours . . ."

"Ask and it shall be given to you . . ."

"All authority has been given to me, Go . . ."

So you're only human, but God can lift you out of the commonplace to a level of glory and wonder and real service to the Lord and His people, if you will dedicate yourself to Him and draw on the resources of heaven to which you have access. Use them and live!

L. M. G.

CONTENTS

In the Appendix there are devotional helps for using this book in organization meetings. Supplemental Scripture, prayer and hymn suggestions especially selected for each chapter are included.

ANY HOLES IN YOUR HEAD?

"FOR THE HOLE in your head when you blow your top" read the card tucked in with one of the most unusual Christmas gifts I have ever received. It was an ordinary large bottle-stopper type cork that had been trimmed with colorful sequins, nestled in tissue in a plastic box and gift-wrapped like a piece of jewelry. It was a clever and effective reminder that when I "blow my top" in a fit of temper, it is I who get the headache.

We think we are entitled to "let off steam" occasionally to relieve our tensions. It is true that the pressure from many demands upon our time and energy, and the heat from the constant friction of dealing with different personalities in a busy life do bring us occasionally to the boiling point where something has to give. Because of the possibility of serious mental or emotional damage from pent-up cumulative tensions, psychology has recognized this fact and has suggested outlets that are safe.

This pressure that builds up within us actually is a tremendous store of energy that can be expelled and dissipated in one terrible burst of temper, or it could possibly be channeled into some creative avenue, or it could be burned off in some form of strenuous work or physical exercise.

Some people have found that when they get to the "exploding point," a good brisk walk, or mowing the lawn, or vigorously scrubbing a floor provides an adequate safety valve. The trick is to recognize when the danger point is near and to turn that emotional energy into safe and constructive channels, if possible.

It is well to remember that if we "let off steam" in an emotional outburst, an innocent bystander is apt to get burned. Certainly when the tirade is directed at another person, it is scorching and searing in its effect, but perhaps its worst by-product is what happens to that person's opinion of the one who is giving vent to his feelings. Anyone who grants himself the indulgence of a temper tantrum automatically lowers himself in the esteem of those who witness the shameful display. Bad temper is actually a nauseous concoction of self-pity, jealousy, impatience, intolerance, and lack of love.

Temper has been called the "vice of the virtuous" because so many otherwise highly moral, fine-principled people lose control of themselves under stress. It becomes the one dark blot on an otherwise admirable character. In an unguarded moment, a thoughtlessly spewed-out word reveals the true nature of the disposition, which may have been quite carefully camouflaged.

Perhaps the reason that this is so common a thing with many people is that we excuse it with the plea that we are born with a particular type of disposition and there isn't a great deal we can do about it. So are we born with appetites of various kinds—and if any of them is allowed to dominate a life, that life is apt to become a grotesque thing. Some people find it naturally easier to be placid and even-tempered than others. Some people do not have to struggle with ungovernable appetites, either.

If we would be Christ-like, we must recognize that the sins of the disposition are as serious and as deadly as the sins of the body and they need the same kind of treatment: repentance and confession and trust in the forgiveness that Christ alone can give. With His forgiveness He will always offer grace and strength to overcome recurring temptations that plague us, until they cease to be a problem. It requires of us only the will to get control of those powerful emotions which can be so great a blessing or so wicked a weapon.

Do you have any holes in your head?

STRAIGHT DOWN THE MIDDLE

A MILD-MANNERED, gentle soul stood before the judge under indictment for murder. One after another, witnesses had testified in his behalf, stating, "The charge is preposterous. This man has never even killed a fly."

"Guilty as charged," the judge declared. "The flies he didn't kill have contaminated the entire city!"

This little fable, though somewhat far-fetched, serves to illustrate the fact that neglecting to do that which is good, right, and necessary (theology would call this the "sin of omission") is often as dangerous and downright evil as deliberate acts of wrong (sins of "commission").

It is often the "Do Nothing" people who sit in judgment upon those who blunder ahead but get things done. They criticize what others are doing when they are neither willing nor able to make a better contribution. They find it much easier to point a finger than to lift one. They are immune from making mistakes because they don't do anything to risk making them.

Another story—and this time a true one—about two little old ladies who returned from a motor trip all upset about the discourtesy of the other drivers.

One of them, firmly convinced that she had the clue to the high accident rate, reported:

"People kept honking their horns at us all the time, and we were the safest drivers. We never drove over thirty-five miles an hour straight down the middle of the road. There was no danger of *our* going in the ditch!"

Carrying caution to the extreme, with no chances taken for fear of making a mistake, is the foolishness of those of little faith who concentrate on life's limitations so that they do not see life's tremendous possibilities.

Such thinking is behind the philosophy that since it is impossible to live perfectly in a covenant relationship with God, it is better never to make a public avowal of allegiance to Him.

A child would never learn to walk if his first frustrating efforts were to discourage him. Each time he picks himself up from a fall he is a little closer to mastering the fine art of walking erect and purposefully. Of course, if he never stood up, he would never fall— but neither would he learn to walk. And walk we must, as Paul told the Ephesians, and he added "look carefully then how you walk, not as unwise but as wise, making the most of the time because the days are evil."

We ought never to measure our progress along the Christian way by what we have not risked, but rather by what we have done that nobody but a Christian would dare to do.

Did you kill any flies today?

HOW COME?

"How come," they ask, "a pretty girl like you has never married?"

If the girl is really pretty, she, too, wonders "how come?" If she is not especially attractive, and knows it, this dubious compliment may push her into the mire of self-pity.

What may have been only a haunting suspicion becomes a certainty in her tortured heart. She is convinced she must be unlovely and must have serious personality faults. She is sure that as a punishment for her lack of these highly prized qualities, she is doomed to live the single life.

To her it may seem some monstrously cruel joke that God, who created male and female and ordained that they should be one flesh for mutual satisfaction and procreation, has destined that she must go through life like a half-person, lonely and incomplete.

There doesn't seem to be any sure formula or combination of assets that guarantees the finding of a mate. It is obviously not true that only pretty women and handsome men marry, although a subtle conspiracy fostered by advertisers has spread the propaganda that physical charm is the magic wand that opens the door to matrimony.

A television comedian not long ago put a new twist on one of the standard advertising blurbs: "She's lovely, she's engaged, she uses Ponds—if she had used soap she would have been married years ago!"

Whether it comes in bottle, jar, or bar—charm, according to the hucksters, is an easily purchased commodity.

Of course, love is not blind to physical beauty. Every woman (and every man, too) has an obligation to make the most of all God-given gifts. Beauty that is "soul-deep" is well mannered, soft spoken, and considerate. It includes common sense, naturalness, unselfish interest in others, and a genuine desire to develop talents and endowments because of what they can do for self, for others, and for the glory of God.

If nature hasn't bestowed glamorous beauty, don't bemoan your plain features as an unhappy discrimination against you. There is satisfactory compensation in the strength of character you can develop and which you can reflect in a cheerful, intelligent poise and bearing.

A real person with warmth, wholesomeness, and depth of genuine character does not emerge like a genie from a jar of cream, a bottle of scent, or even a bar of soap.

Many women actually suffer from a sense of inferiority because they have not married. They feel isolated from a society based largely on the family unit. Having become convinced that marriage is the only goal in life that counts, they check themselves off as total failures. They fret about their single status until their personalities become warped. Their mental and emotional attitudes color and distort their pattern of behavior until some of them become as queer, in many ways, as the ridiculous "old maid" of the comic strips.

Marriage does not *ipso facto* make anyone happy, nor does remaining single guarantee happiness. It is possible to achieve happiness in either state if the most is made of the opportunities God gives.

It is no tragedy to be single—it is only a tragedy to have failed to adjust to being single!

NO REQUEST REFUSED

"GIVE TO EVERY man that asketh of thee; and of him that taketh away thy goods ask them not again" (Luke 6:30).

Have you ever wondered what might happen if you followed this admonition to the letter?

What do you think you would have left if word got around that you would refuse no request?

In *Men as Trees Walking*, Miss Margaret Applegarth tells what happened when a young missionary stumbled onto these words while teaching his black people who were gathered in a circle on the ground around him.

For four years he had been looking for some change in the lives of the natives as he had tried to teach them about God. The black heads would nod approvingly as he taught, but they continued to be the same people, people who often at night would steal the much-coveted possessions of the missionary. He realized that somehow he had to make them understand the love of Jesus Christ, so he decided to translate for them the Gospel of Luke.

As he neared the thirtieth verse of the sixth chapter, he debated with himself whether God would under-

9

stand if he skipped that particular verse because he couldn't figure out how to explain to the natives what was really meant by: "Give to every man that asketh of thee; and of him that taketh away thy goods ask them not again." He was afraid that the people would interpret it as an open invitation to loot him of all his meager possessions. Perhaps this portion of the Word of God would do more harm than good.

Finally the young missionary decided that this was no less God's Word than any of the rest of the Bible and he had no right to withhold even a few words.

His worst fears were realized, for he had barely finished his translation when his listeners, with a great wild shout, descended upon his home and the "Great Grab" was on.

There was jubilant revelry for hours, but eventually the mirth subsided and they lay down to rest, surrounded with their new treasures. In the still of the night, consciences, which had been introduced to Jesus Christ, began to talk back to them. They remembered the young man of God who had stood silent and alone as they snatched the things which represented his only contact with his homeland. Silently the procession began, moving from the huts to the missionary's cottage, returning the stolen articles. The young man who had been able to relinquish even valued personal possessions without protest, had given them a vivid demonstration of the unselfish love of Christ. They were not apt to forget the lesson.

God can be taken at His Word—His full Word. Although it may seem contrary to good sense, it can be lived. To follow God's directions to the letter may result in a temporary reversal of fortune, but a greater victory may be achieved when the miracle of Christ's love dawns on those who witness it in action.

"Give to every man that asketh of thee; and of him that taketh thy goods ask them not again."

If we are possessed by our possessions, this is a hard saying to accept. When we have the grace to acknowledge that we possess nothing, we may miraculously find it possible to say, "No request will be refused."

HE MADE NO ANSWER

DURING THE LENTEN season as attention is focused again upon the familiar scene of the "trial" of Jesus before Pilate, it seems to me that one amazing thing about it is the remarkable poise and self-control of our Lord.

It was evidently something unique in the experience of Pilate, too, for the Gospels relate that he "wondered greatly" at this Man who could hold His peace in the face of such flagrant injustice. Pilate acted against his own better judgment and allowed himself to play a part in this farce, but he "wondered greatly" that it drew no reaction from his victim.

It was not an insolent silence. It was not sullen. The silence of Jesus before Pilate was eloquent, infuriating the mob because it condemned them more certainly than any words could have.

Matthew reports the incident thus:

"Now Jesus stood before the governor; and the governor asked him, 'Are you the King of the Jews?' Jesus said to him, 'You have said so.' But when he was accused by the chief priests and elders, he made no answer. Then Pilate said to him, 'Do you not hear how many things they testify against you?' But he gave him no answer, not even to a single charge; so that the governor wondered greatly" (27:11-14).

It may be hard to reconcile this meek and mild Jesus, who patiently endured persecution, with the Jesus who purged the temple, assaulted the greedy merchants, and threw them into the street. He is the same Jesus who on occasion insulted the sanctimonious clergy and called them hypocrites. He trod roughshod over their sacrosanct regulations and empty rituals. It was not lack of character or strength of personality that rendered Him dumb before His accusers, for He was a most virile and dynamic person.

In this instance, however, His silence was His strongest defense. He knew that these events must happen. He knew also that His Father could transform these wrongs into the one great right by which even His tormentors could be redeemed for eternity.

Had He kept silent in the temple when He came upon the money changers, His silence would have been tantamount to approval of the contamination of that holy place. On the other hand, to give the baseless accusations of the chief priests and elders the dignity of an answer would have added fuel to a raging, directionless fire.

Oh, for the mind of Christ to know when silence is the better part of wisdom!

Our natural tendency is to "tell off" unjust accusers. If we don't assert our rights someone is going to "push us around" or "walk all over us." Just possibly we might come off second best or appear to have been made a "sucker." To avoid that, we shoot off our mouths and thereby prove conclusively what type of fools we really are.

Declaring our right to save face, usually becomes a miserable process that does damage all around, causes misunderstandings, creates bad feelings, fosters grudges, and in the end makes us appear smaller in the eyes of our fellowmen.

Is it worth it—just to salvage our pride?

If we would be like Jesus, this is another lesson we can learn from Him.

The beloved old Negro spiritual expresses it thus: "And He never said a mumblin' word!"

That's real greatness!

HOW BIG ARE YOU?

MOST PEOPLE HAVE a pretty good idea of how tall they are and how much they weigh, although they may be reluctant to admit it. Some consider the excess poundage they carry one of life's greatest burdens. The tall ones grind their heels into the ground and slump to appear shorter. The short ones wear elevated shoes to stretch them a little higher. The thin ones resort to padding and bulky clothing to create the illusion of more "acceptable" figures. The length of bone and the amount of flesh which provide temporary covering for our immortal souls seem to take on greater importance than the real person that dwells within our imperfect frames.

Perhaps it was with a view to turning our attention a little away from our physical bodies that Jesus said in the Sermon on the Mount, "which of you by taking thought can add one cubit unto his stature?"

How big is the *real* you?

To take a measurement of the "inner man" may not seem an easy trick, but we can use that familiar trio of graces: faith, hope, and love as a rule to determine the true stature of a Christian.

How deep is your faith in Christ?

How high is your hope of heaven?

How wide is your love for others?

Does your spirit, which is the real you, reach Christ-ward in trust, man-ward in concern, and heaven-ward in confidence?

There isn't much chance of adding to our physical height, but there is plenty of Scriptural evidence that we can and must "grow in grace of the knowledge of God." Such growth takes place when we are being properly nourished on the Word, where we gain some comprehension of His will, catch an insight into the nature of Christ, become alert to the needs of men, and appreciate the nearness of heaven. The result ought to be healthy steady growth in a life of useful service.

We don't need to be spiritual pygmies. We can be "giants in the earth"—full-grown, mature Christians.

Have you taken your measurements recently?

How big are you?

SINGING IN THE CRACKS

A WOMAN WHO HAD a consuming desire to become a great singer hired the best teacher available. After some time working with her, the teacher said one day, "I am sorry, but I can no longer have you as a pupil. I play on the black keys and I play on the white keys but you persist in singing in the cracks!"

There are people like that who sing in the cracks of life. They are neither positive nor negative personalities. They are just flabby. They vacillate from one thing to another because they have no inner unity or consistency. They are not what we would call "integrated personalities." They lack direction and purpose because they haven't yet found anything more important to worry about than themselves.

It is extremely important to be an integrated personality with inner cohesion, because disintegration is madness. Insanity is the complete lack of consistency in the personality.

The best way to achieve an integrated personality is to establish a dominant purpose in life and then with God's help turn the entire will toward its accomplishment. In that way the scattered forces of personality can be drawn together and unified into a drive toward the desired goal.

Of course it is possible to accomplish this on various moral levels. If the resulting strong personality is to be admirable, the purpose must be worthy or the end result may be moral collapse, and that is fully as bad as disintegration.

The world offers many alternatives and holds up a number of attractive goals which tantalize. It has wealth, power, fame to offer to anyone who will pay the price. Strangely enough—or perhaps it is not so strange, considering the affinity there is between the world and the devil—those goals are strongly reminiscent of the temptations that the devil set before Jesus in the wilderness. The price might well be the same: a man's soul. Undoubtedly untold numbers of people have paid that price for the transient pleasure of the prize.

The Bible suggests a worthy objective. "Seek first the Kingdom of God and His righteousness, and all these things will be added unto you."

There is constant conflict between our natural tendency toward evil and the good that we know we should do. The flesh and the spirit are endlessly struggling for supremacy. Paul had the same problem. He said "For I know that nothing good dwells within me, that is, in my flesh. I can will what is right, but I cannot do it. For I do not do the good I want, but the evil I do not want is what I do."

It isn't easy to bring about a balance between the standards of the social group in which we live and the way of life delineated by the Word of God. "Singing in the cracks" is a grueling, tortuous and nerve-wracking experience for everyone concerned, but we can be in tune with the infinite and keep the pitch if, like Peter when he walked on the water, we keep our attention off ourselves and on Jesus. Then we can move through each day with perfect poise and confidence as perfectly balanced, integrated personalities.

ACT YOUR AGE

HAVE YOU SEEN grown people sulk when their ideas are rebuffed or ignored? Have you seen women burst into tears of rage, or frustration, over minor matters? Have you been exposed to the sensitive type who "flies off the handle" at the least provocation? Have you been embarrassed in a public place when a companion has peevishly whined (usually in a loud voice) that someone else has been served out of turn though it meant a delay of only a few seconds? Have you heard a man complain that his wife doesn't understand him? Have you watched middle-aged men attempt to recapture their youth by cutting loose at a convention and engaging in idiotic and dangerous "horseplay"?

These people are emotionally immature. They are reacting to situations according to behavior patterns established in childhood. Tears and tantrums and public demonstrations may bring the desired results, but are certainly a shameful exhibition of a warped and stunted personality.

The tragedy of emotionally immature people is that they have reached adulthood physically and mentally and have every chance of living a normal balanced life but their emotional development has stopped at the infantile level. They have never progressed beyond the juvenile concern for "me too" in every situation. Personal gratification, comfort, convenience, and appeasement of their own appetites are the guiding principles behind their every act. They don't care how rude they may be or whose feelings may be hurt by their actions. They don't seem even to be aware of the people about them except as it affects them personally. They are difficult to live with. They are touchy, easily upset and are not above throwing tantrums over trivialities.

Emotional immaturity is a pathetic abnormality because for the most part it is the result of pure selfishness. They just refuse to act their age.

Too many of us, who consider ourselves emotionally

mature, at times act as though we had only one obligation and that was to ourselves. As long as we don't deliberately harm anyone else or become a burden to them, we ought to be able to live and let live. But that narrow kind of existence doesn't fit into the social structure of interdependence between human beings. There can be no emotional growth when all our actions are directed toward self. Those who become overly concerned for self-gratification, self-pity, and self-interest of various kinds soon become misfits in society, unable to cope with normal responsibilities.

Real maturity is moving out of oneself, entering into and sharing the problems, concerns, joys, and sorrows of others through sympathetic participation, cooperation, and compassion. Real maturity is expanding self-interests to include others, even to the extent of considering their rights and happiness above our own.

There is one sure cure for emotional immaturity— that is simply to act your age!

Paul outlined such a program for the Philippians "Do nothing from selfishness or conceit, but in humility count others better than yourselves. Let each of you look not only to his own interests, but also to the interests of others."

LOST AND FOUND

THERE IS A STRANGE paradox in the teachings of Jesus which affirms that he that loses his life shall find it. He did that. It wasn't easy, but He proved it could be done.

Jesus contributed His philosophy of life to an already complex assortment of philosophies, but He demonstrated how it works for peace, happiness, and ultimate victory over life's tribulations. He lived on man's level with all of its pitfalls and, as a man, showed us it is practical and possible to love God and our fellowmen.

He met disappointment, scorn, treachery, and deceit, but it never made Him cynical or discouraged. He endured cruelty of the most fiendish type. He suffered untold physical and mental anguish, but His reaction was forgiveness, not resentment. He never expressed any desire for revenge, nor did He appear to feel sorry for Himself. He was deserted by friends, family, and even by God, it seemed, but His faith in the constancy of His mission and purpose in life did not waver. He was the perfect example of the mature, balanced personality. He experienced the whole range of emotion and controlled it. He wept for a dead friend and for a doomed city. He was aroused to active anger over the desecration of a holy place. He suffered hunger, thirst, weariness, and loneliness. He sweat huge drops of blood and He died in disgrace, but it was His oppressors who cowered in fear. It was His enemies who struck out blindly in a futile gesture against the few friends who knew that although He lived and died as a man, He was also God.

Time and again Jesus invited the interested and the curious to come and see, to follow, and to learn of Him as He moved among them. He set the path and blazed the trail. It is possible to follow in His steps.

His plan calls for an outreach toward others. We can't do that if we cloister ourselves and ignore the rest of the world. We must serve both the Lord and His people. If we would find life, we must lose ourselves to it.

We can live life in this stride, meeting its problems, disappointments and frustrations with equanimity if we let Christ's kind of unselfish love permeate our personalities. In that way we can stand outside of our narrow little selves and act in terms of the common good with complete freedom from personal bias, petty ego-centric needs, prejudice, or anticipation of reward.

"Have this mind among yourselves, which you have in Christ Jesus, who, though He was in the form of God, did not count equality with God a thing to be grasped, but emptied Himself, taking the form of a servant, being born in the likeness of men."

We don't have much to lose if we lose our lives in order to find life. Jesus was willing and did forego the glory of being on an equality with God in order to serve mankind. To be able to lose ourselves that completely is really to find ourselves.

Meditation

THINK

IN AN OFFICE WHERE I once worked we had a motto with only one well-chosen word on it. That word was THINK. The motto had been the gift of the International Business Machines Corporation, manufacturers of one of the amazing so-called "electronic brains" and other tabulating, computing machines and office equipment.

This corporation also publishes and distributes to its customers a monthly slick paper magazine which they call THINK. Although you would expect otherwise, the magazine contains no advertising. It is a carefully selected and edited compilation of interesting articles on cultural, educational, and religious subjects.

Of course, both the motto and the magazine are advertising gimmicks for the IBM Corporation, but the impact is effective and they are well calculated to stimulate the reader to think.

It seemed a little curious to me that a corporation, whose business is producing gadgets especially designed to take the strain off the human mind, should use such a method and catch phrase to draw attention to itself.

The word THINK focuses not on machinery which is their product, but on the human being and his remarkable powers of perception. The valuable material in the magazine is for the edification and enjoyment of the operators of the machinery and those who plan and direct the work.

When I learned that the chairman of the board of the IBM Corporation is a Christian gentleman whose personal faith, ideals, and principles of business administration have set the tone for the whole corporation, I began to understand why a huge impersonal corporation would have such concern for that most god-like of all human characteristics: our ability to think.

We are fearfully and wonderfully made—created in the image of God and endowed with the power to use our mentalities. We are not like machines, geared and adjusted to produce predictable results. And we won't become robots or mechanical men, responding only to external stimulation, if we use our capacity to observe the world around us, study the facts, weigh and consider one in relation to another and arrive at our own independent conclusions.

We may not be able to control everything that happens to us, but we are capable of independent judgments and advance planning so that to a large extent we can determine our own destiny. That is what makes it so important that we develop our powers to think and use them well.

The quality of a man's thought-life is one measure of his character: "As a man thinketh in his heart, so is he."

FRAGMENTATION

MANY TIMES I FALL exhausted into bed at night knowing that although I have made many decisions during the day, the hectic pace has kept me rushing from one task to another and there has been no time for any real meditation.

I drop off to sleep, promising myself that tomorrow will be better. I will cut down somewhere so that I can do some reading. I will try to absorb some of the finer things of life. I will make time to sort out ideas and decide what to do with them. But while I realize that my life is being impoverished because I don't get around to doing the things which will improve my mind, these fine resolutions, like so many others, fall by the wayside. It is a discouraging note on which to end the day.

There are so many distractions, so much noise, so many demands clamoring for attention all the time that it is difficult to achieve any kind of balance in the midst of these contradictory tensions. Life in America for the average person is based on maintaining innumerable contacts in many important and varied areas. There are the demands of our work, our families, our social and cultural world. As good citizens we should keep abreast of world events, develop some opinions on politics, and participate to some extent in civic activities. We must cooperate with the educational system where possible. We must serve our Lord in His church and the many organizations which aim to do His work. We must support worthy charitable appeals.

The multiple pulls on our time, our energy, and our financial resources naturally lead to fragmentation. Our interests and our duties reach out in many directions, yet somehow in the midst of all this we must remain whole. To set aside occasionally a time for quiet solitary meditation may help to pull it all together and at the same time renew our strength and our inspiration. The most aggressive army must occasionally retreat to regroup.

To most housewives and mothers who daily face a sinkful of dirty dishes, unmade beds, laundry piled high, a baby who must be tended and who clamors constantly for attention, the suggestion that some time ought to be dedicated to private meditation, may sound quite impossible, if not utterly ridiculous.

Nor is it any easier for a career woman who must bring order out of her life, taking care of her home (and every woman—whether married or single—must make some kind of home), meeting the demands of her job, society, and church. The career woman often finds herself at the end of a weary day, lugging a bag of groceries onto a crowded bus, seeing ahead a full evening of more work at home to prepare for the next day's battle with industry to pay the rent, and knowing that there hasn't been and isn't apt to be a moment in which she can enrich her life through meditation. In her crowded day, too, it is not easy.

It isn't easy for any of us, but because of our very nature, which is to give of ourselves constantly in whatever we do, it is an absolute essential that we find a chance to refresh our minds and replenish our spirits through some form of stimulating mental and spiritual exercise if we are to continue another day to give of ourselves to those who depend on us.

Is there an answer? Perhaps not, but there is a good suggestion in what Thomas à Kempis wrote in his little book *Of the Imitation of Christ*: "If thou wilt withdraw thyself from speaking vainly and gadding idly, as also from hearkening after novelties and rumors, thou shalt find leisure enough and suitable for meditation on good things."

ON THESE THINGS

SOMEONE HAS SAID that ideas have legs and ideas come of thinking. Things get done quicker, better, and with more effectiveness when they have been thought through and prayed over.

People who don't think are like water running down a hill. They follow the paths of least resistance. They conform to the ruts already worn deep by others who have gone the same way.

To conform all the time is one form of adolescence. The mature person fearlessly formulates his own ideas on the basis of his own sound judgment after intelligent consideration. He may be radically different from his neighbors, but he may be the one who contributes something significant to life for having spent some time thinking through some of the problems of life.

Conformists did not make America what it is today. The conformists in American history have been forgotten because they did so little to make the United States the great nation that it is. It was the innovators, the people who thought, the people who read books, who put their thoughts into action, who did it.

A great many things can claim our attention—some not worthy of the effort. There are all kinds of books to read, many types of programs offered on radio and television, lectures, movies, drama—a vast offering of educational and cultural entertainment, but a large amount also of just plain trash. We must make a choice, for our time is naturally limited and we must decide what will help us develop our minds and the ideas which take legs and go places for us.

What we think about is governed to a large extent by what we see, read, and otherwise absorb. In making the choice of what to think about, we can use Paul's formula suggested to the Philippians: "Whatever is honorable, whatever is just, whatever is pure, whatever is lovely, whatever is gracious, if there is any excellence, if there is anything worthy of praise, think on these things."

BURIED TALENT

ANYONE WHO HAS studied Latin will remember something about Cicero. He was a brilliant, capable man, very handsome, charming, and dashing. In fact, he was all that a man in his time needed to be in order to be a significant success among the Romans.

Caesar was another such brilliant, talented young man. He was equally handsome. He was eloquent and socially poised. But Caesar possessed in addition a certain military genius which brought him more and more into the public eye. There was quite naturally a strong feeling of competition between Cicero and Caesar, and Cicero began to fear he was losing some of his popularity by comparison, because, in the area of his military prowess, Caesar was one jump ahead of him.

Cicero, while he might have continued to hold a reasonable measure of public esteem, became obsessed with jealousy. Every chance he had, he attacked the moral character of Caesar. He no longer spoke easily in public. He became moody, suspicious, and withdrawn. He acted as though by tearing Caesar down he would restore himself to first place in the opinion of the

31

public. He was so bitter in his obvious envy of Caesar's superior talent that eventually he lost his appeal for the people because of the drastic change that had occurred in his personality. The canker of jealousy gnawed at him until he became a cantankerous, bitter old man. His fear of losing popularity because of the inadequacy of his talent had backfired. It robbed him of what he had.

Jesus dealt with the problem when He told the disciples the parable of the talents. It is a familiar story. A master gave to one of his servants five talents, two to another, and one to the third. Later he returned and inquired how they had used the talents they had been given. He found the first two had increased theirs through wise investment and sensible use. The third servant could only whimper, "I was afraid, so I went and buried my talent."

This servant, who was afraid of the inadequacy of his talent, didn't use it at all. He just dug it down deep to keep it safe! But his plan backfired, too. The master took from him the talent he had been given.

While we realize, of course, that the "talent" of the parable was a piece of currency, the same basic principle holds in the area of our abilities which we commonly refer to as "talents."

By nature all of us don't have the same abilities, nor can we all serve our Lord and His Kingdom in the same way. That fact, too, has been made clear in Scripture. We have diversified talents, but we all have some. If we do not use them, or if we burn ourselves up in bitterness and jealousy because they are not identical with those of everyone else, we will lose what we have.

Talent never comes to anyone full-blown. It has to be nourished, cultivated, and used in order to increase! We ought not to be afraid to launch out and use the talent we have.

It is actually an affront to God, the giver of talents, to deny that we have them. It may take a measure of raw courage to step out and try what we suspect may be a talent, however undeveloped it is. But only by wise investment can our talents increase and we make any significant contributions to life with them.

Very likely Peter never suspected he had a "talent" for walking on the water. He just tried it and he could. Perhaps, in his case it was not so much a "talent" as it was an unquestioning confidence in the Word of his Master. It takes that kind of confident obedience for us to try to do some things that seem equally ridiculous or impossible. As long as Peter kept his eye on the Lord he did all right. When he said to himself, "Well, Peter, look at yourself! You are better than you thought. You can walk on the water!" he began to sink.

Paul, too, learned from his own experience that he

could "do all things through Christ who strengthens me."

We have not all been endowed with great talents. We may be endowed with feeble little inclinations that we perhaps only sense because of a slightly intensified interest in one area or another. Even the talent that we scarcely recognize, has not been given to us for foolish or flippant or selfish purposes. All the power of the Kingdom of God stands behind and aids the talents intended to do great things for God—into whatever field of endeavor we are guided.

We attribute our fear of the inadequacy of our talents to "modesty." Actually it may be a combination of laziness and indifference that prevents our using them. Fear of any sort is enervating. It is responsible for most of life's failures. Fear shears us of vitality, weakens our moral fiber, and works havoc with the health of both our minds and bodies. It is one of the devil's most useful tools for reducing strong people to sniveling weaklings.

While the public may acclaim one talent as of greater value than another, the world's standards of value are not always reliable.

To do the will of God in the way He indicates, is the best possible use of talent. God does not put "degrees" on our talents. He measures how faithfully we use them.

PUBLIC OPINION

No ONE KNOWS better than the parents of teen-agers how important conforming to gang standards seems to be. These young people must wear what everyone else wears, however disreputable. They must speak the same jargon, whether intelligible or not. They must do everything according to the accepted pattern. It is almost impossible for parents to keep up with what is "just right" at the moment because these rigid standards undergo drastic changes quickly for no apparent reason. The fear of deviating in the slightest degree from the current fad becomes a real problem for the very young.

Some adults never get beyond this adolescent stage. They continue through life conforming and following the mob wherever it may lead. They haven't the courage to strike out independently. They do not attempt to follow a personal conviction to its conclusion because they are afraid of public opinion.

I believe it was fear of public opinion that caused Peter to deny his Lord. Jesus was not popular at that moment. He was being dragged off in disgrace by the soldiers. Suddenly it seemed the most important thing in the world for Peter to avoid being identified with Him for fear the mob would turn on him next. He was so sensitive to the taunts of the people and so afraid of their scorn that he was ready to give up everything he had learned about the reality of the Kingdom of God. He, who had vowed faithfully to stand by his Master, resorted to profanity to underline his denial of any connection with Him whatsoever.

That easily the fear of the opinion of others can sway us away from a noble purpose of life.

Then the dawn came for Peter. It came literally when the cock's crowing sharply recalled his mind from the paralysis of his fear. He remembered that Jesus had warned him that before the cock should crow Peter would deny Him three times. As his conscious mind regained control, he became aware of the enormity of his denial. Fortunately for Peter and for the future of the Christian church as well, at that point he made a wise decision. In real repentence he asked for and received forgiveness. He was ever after that a stronger man for the experience.

By contrast to the Peter who cringed in fear of the opinion of a handful of servants, we see another picture of him at Pentecost, boldly standing before a hostile crowd loudly jeering and accusing him and the other disciples of being drunk or insane. The Peter of Pentecost, filled with the power of the Holy Ghost and with the sure knowledge of the risen Lord Jesus Christ, was no longer afraid of public opinion or anything else, because he had a message that must be told. He told them "there is salvation in no one else, for there is no other name under heaven given among men by which we must be saved."

It is written that the people could see that "they had been with Jesus" and they "had nothing to say in opposition." Three thousand souls were added to the Kingdom as a result of Peter's fearless presentation of the truth.

Peter, himself, explained his courage when he said ". . . we cannot but speak of what we have seen and heard."

If the fear of public opinion stops your mouth when you ought to speak for the sake of justice or truth, then you have not seen or heard what God has done, or you do not know personally what forgiveness can mean.

Many of us lose the thrill of living vigorous, effective, victorious lives because we are afraid to appear odd. The world lives by the law of greed, lust, and selfishness and has thereby precipitated the present state of chaos and conflict. Any sane, thinking person who doesn't let fear detach his mind from his body should be able to see that living by the law of love is the superior way.

Are you afraid to be different, even though you are right? Why should you fear the opinion of others? To whom will you have to render an account of your life?

You are not responsible to your fellowmen. You are responsible to God. If God be for you, who can be against you?

A WARM BOTTLE

I watched a small boy run the length of the dock and throw himself off into space. The water was deep. I knew the boy could not swim, but I was not concerned for his safety. His father stood in the water at the end of the dock. Each time the child came flying through the air, the father would catch him, splash around in the water with him and then toss him back onto the dock where the whole process would be repeated. From the hilarious laughter, it was evident that the little boy was not the least bit afraid.

A baby very early develops a fear of hunger. When its pangs grip him, he reacts in the only way he knows: he cries. Soon he learns that when he cries he gets fed and when he has been fed the hunger disappears. Gradually he develops a trust in the lady who comes to his crib with a warm bottle.

These little ones who can overcome their basic fears and replace them with trust and confidence in father and mother to protect and to feed them, make adults who fret about insecurity seem rather ridiculous. Even after many years of having their daily needs satisfied and having experienced in so many ways that the Heavenly Father protects them from danger and from hunger, they still have not learned to trust Him for their security.

It is easy to fall into the habit of depending on things, believing them to be solid and immutable. If we just have enough money, a good house, a reasonably new car, and clothes, nothing can touch us, we think. Yet we have seen people who had all these things in abundance suddenly made destitute and dependent upon the charity of others when a disaster strikes. A fire, in a matter of minutes, can reduce their solid security to a worthless heap of smoldering ashes. A tornado can change a prosperous residential area into a shambles.

Some people surround themselves with worldly goods, bar the doors, and spend their lives guarding their possessions. For them, the fear of insecurity has become a senseless obsession. They get neither pleasure nor utility from their possessions. The more dependent we become upon things for our security, the more enslaved we are to fear.

We say, "Every man for himself" and, "I'm going to get mine while I can." Our attitude about security grows from need to greed. We want more and more for ourselves, and become convinced that we actually require that much. Sometimes we resort to varying degrees of dishonesty and violence to increase our holdings—because we are afraid of insecurity.

We are afraid to share what we have with others. We do not see that our benevolence may be a blessing to us as well as to those who receive it. Some of us when forced by circumstances to part with anything, feel that the only result has been a huge hole in the dike of our personal security.

The rich young ruler who came to Jesus to be assured of eternal life was asked if he had kept the commandments. He said he had. Jesus said, ". . . then there is one thing more that is necessary, go and sell all that you have and give it to the poor."

This was a shocking request. The young man was very wealthy and he was accustomed to wealth. This requirement would mean quite a drastic change in his life. How could he exist without his possessions? He did not recognize that Jesus was not interested in impoverishing the young man, He only wanted to test his trust.

The young man took his own measure and decided he wasn't big enough to stand without the props that his wealth provided.

Jesus never intended us to be reckless and unwise in the use of possessions. He expects us to work hard to achieve the means of supporting ourselves and our dependents and to plan carefully for the future. Amassing a fortune, of whatever size, however, must not become our sole reason for existence.

Tithing is still one of God's laws. He expects at least ten percent of our income to be turned back to His purposes—not because He needs it, but because He has chosen this means of involving us in Kingdom work and because we need to comprehend the necessity for relaxing our hold on what has been given to us. Better to have ninety percent of what we earn with God's blessing on it than the full one hundred percent without His benediction.

Fear of insecurity is one of the most flagrant denials of our professed faith in the Heavenly Father. Has He not promised to care for what He has created? Paul's experience was that "My God shall supply every need of yours according to His riches in glory through Christ Jesus."

GRIM REAPER

IF WE COULD CONCEIVE of a person absolutely devoid of any fear, that person would be in constant danger, for a certain amount of fear is necessary for precautionary purposes.

Jesus said "Take heed you who stand lest you fall." If, however, we are so afraid of the possibility of falling that we don't try to stand up, then we have carried caution to a ridiculous extreme.

It is evident from Scripture that God expects us to react fearfully to certain things. All the way through the Bible there are repeated admonitions from the Lord to "fear not" and "be not afraid" and "let not your heart be troubled." It seems that every time God displayed His supernatural power before men, He prefaced the manifestation with that warning. We can draw courage from the fact that in every instance when God said "be not afraid" there actually was no cause for fear.

When Jesus sent the disciples out to witness for Him, He warned them not to be afraid of the strange things they would encounter or of the unpredictable reactions of the people they would meet.

Man fears unknown things, and especially the future that he has tried in vain to fathom and is unable to understand.

Most of our fear of the future resolves itself into three categories; fear of old age and resultant illness or disability; fear of possible insecurity; and fear of death and eternity.

Of the three, only death and eternity is inevitable. We may not live to old age. We may never become seriously ill or infirm. We may never know poverty, but death will come for all.

Some people consider the subject of death so morbid that they refuse to discuss it. It is as though they thought by evading the issue they could escape it.

Of course, if a man is healthy, life is good. Regardless of age, death is an unwelcome intruder. Actually, fear of death is only the result of a natural instinct for self-preservation, and the physical fact of dying seems tantamount to destruction.

It is a fearsome thing to see what a ghastly transformation a long period of suffering can make in one who is ill. But medics say that the so-called "agony" of death is felt far more keenly by the bedside observers than by the one who is dying. There is a blessed numbness that blunts the feeling. In spite of long suffering in illness, the last moments and the actual dying is free from pain. After all, "He knoweth our frame. He remembers that we are dust."

In considering departure from this life, we fear the finality of it all. We don't like to think that everything we have accomplished, everything we have aspired toward, everything we love, our ideals, and everything that makes up the sum total of life will one day end in a hole in the ground. We are afraid of total extinction. It is amazing how many people choose to follow that line of reasoning rather than to accept the fact of judgment and everlasting life beyond the grave.

We, who believe Jesus spoke the truth and who know that "He who raised the Lord Jesus will raise us also with Jesus and bring us into His presence," have nothing to fear.

Jesus said, "My peace I leave with you, my peace I give unto you. In my Father's house are many mansions, if it were not so I would have told you. I go to prepare a place for you. . . ." It is as though He were telling us not to worry about the future life.

Death is not an uncharted, undiscovered country from which no traveler has ever returned. Jesus returned, didn't He?

Death, often referred to as a "grim reaper" and an enemy, has only one function, that is to conduct us into the presence of our Heavenly Father. It is like the strange policeman who finds a lost child. He takes the child down a long, dark, unfamiliar hall. The child is terrified at the strangeness—the strange man, the strange place. Then in a room at the other end of the hall is his father. There is love and joy in the face of the father because his child has been returned to him. Safe in his father's arms, the boy wonders why he had been afraid of one who was merely taking him to his father.

The fear of judgment is not so common among people as it once was. We have come to regard God less as a stern father who does not tolerate disobedience, and more as an indulgent grandparent who overlooks our wilfullness and can be won over by our charm. We have a less acute sense of sin and its consequences. There is nothing in Scripture, however, to indicate that God's laws have relaxed their requirements.

Paul said, "There is therefore now no condemnation to them that are in Christ Jesus." The only thing about death that should cause fear is the condemnation that belongs to those who refuse to accept Jesus Christ.

Ultimately we shall all have to acknowledge Jesus Christ as Lord. For some it will be in anguish and sorrow because it is too late.

If we don't know what the future holds for us, we ought to be mighty sure that we know Him who holds the future in His hands. Then the "grim reaper" cannot terrorize us.

A SURE CURE

I WAS PROUD AND HAPPY, but terrified, to have been chosen out of our high school to introduce the guest speaker at convocation. He was an alumnus of our school, a local boy who had "made good." He had studied as a Rhodes scholar at Oxford in England, had traveled widely, had taught in various colleges, and had authored several important articles. We were excited over the prospect of having him speak to our high school when he came home on a visit.

It was my responsibility to meet our guest in the principal's office before the assembly meeting, and to be prepared to introduce him properly to the students.

Perhaps my obvious fright prompted him to say it, but whatever it was, our gracious guest put me at ease almost at once when he said, "I'm scared. Aren't you?" When I admitted I was too, suddenly I discovered I was no longer nearly so frightened as before.

Fear is an emotion that has strong physical manifestations. When we are in its grip, it can dominate action and thought. If we allow it to get control over us, it can become more than an emotion, more than a physical spasm. It can become a false god.

Since fear is such a common affliction and disrupts so much of life, wouldn't it be wonderful if someone would produce and market a sure cure for it?

There are things that will help overcome this numbing, debilitating emotion. First of all, recognize that you are afraid. To admit that gives you the upper hand and a chance to use your head to figure out a solution based on trust in the infinite goodness of God.

Then there are perhaps three basic steps that follow. The first is to *value yourself*. Put a price tag on your life. Ask yourself, "What am I worth to the universe?" Habitual modesty may cause you to underrate your worth, so take a look into Scripture and see how you stand. You will see that you were created in the image of God. You will find that you are only "a little lower than the angels." Can you argue with that evaluation?

Paul understood the value of the human personality. He wrote "He who spared not His own Son, but delivered Him up for us all, how shall He not with Him also freely give us all things?"

We aren't the victims of blind chance. We are the recipients of divine providence.

The second important step in overcoming fear is to *accept yourself*. The comic strip character, Popeye the Sailor, often says, "I yam what I yam and that's all that I yam." Grammatically there is much to be desired in what Popeye says, but Scripture has a similar bit of wisdom:

"Which of you by taking thought can add one cubit to your stature?"

Some things can't be changed. Those things we must learn to accept. Sometimes we chafe under the hardships of life and tend to blame God for burdening us. If you are handicapped in some way, or feel that you got short-changed on talent, good looks, education, or opportunities, are you going to feel sorry for yourself? You must not shrink into the background and spend your life in envy and bitterness because you are not built and equipped as well as someone else. The secret is to be able to find your place in life, unearth your talents and develop them to the fullest possible extent. And it won't hurt to pray, "Lord, help me to accept the things that can't be changed, to change what ought to be changed and to have the wisdom to know the difference."

Jesus accepted His lot in life in the spirit of His prayer "Not my will but thine be done."

The third step to overcoming fear is to *consecrate yourself.*

We usually want to put the cart before the horse. We have a great desire for things, money, pleasure, fame, ease, and the like. But Jesus said "Seek ye first the Kingdom of God and His righteousness and all these things will be added unto you."

We pray, "Thy Kingdom come, but not right now, there are things I want to do for myself first."

We can lose ourselves, and our self-concern—and fear, too, if we consecrate our lives to the service of God and seek first His Kingdom.

If there is any sure cure for fear and worry, it is pretty well outlined in the eighth chapter of Romans which says in part:

"For you did not receive the spirit of slavery to fall back into fear, but you have received the spirit of sonship . . . we know that in everything God works for good with those who love him. . . ."

WHAT TIME IS IT?

IT DIDN'T TAKE the primitive man long to learn that a stick driven into the ground would cast a shadow in the same direction each day when the sun reached a particular position in its apparent journey across the archway of the sky. Later man discovered that it is not the sun which moves across the heavens, but the earth which makes a daily trip around the sun. As he devised more accurate instruments for measuring time, he realized that the daily revolution of the earth made natural time zones all around the world. While he was fascinated by all this, man became aware that he was enslaved by the clock. Now one of his most frequent and urgent inquiries is *What time is it?*" for his whole life is dominated by the hour.

Recently we have further complicated the reckoning of time by a kind of mild deception called "Daylight Saving Time." By transferring an hour from one end of the day to the other, we try to make ourselves believe that we have saved a little daylight.

No amount of manipulation of the hands of the clock, however, can add one minute to the daily twenty four hours. Only God can alter the basic time pattern—He can end it.

Time, as we know it, is an infinitesimal segment of eternity that God has marked off into units that we can understand. It is a gift of God and, as with the other gifts He has given us, we have only temporary control, but we are responsible for its use.

As a gift of God, time is not handed to us in a complete packet to be used at our leisure. It flows relentlessly into and out of our lives. It comes to us regularly, minute by minute. It marches forward in steady unbroken cadence into eternity. Once it has passed us, it is gone forever. It doesn't pause. It doesn't stop. It doesn't wait for us to decide what to do with it. It must be taken when it is here, or it is lost forever.

We can use it or lose it. We can invest it or spend it. We can make it live or we can kill it. But we never get a second chance to use it.

To each is allotted a portion of time and when it ends for us, our opportunity to do God's will in our lifetime is over. "The years of our life are three score and ten, or even by reason of strength fourscore . . . they are soon gone and we fly away."

If juggling the hands of the clock will result in better use of that segment of eternity which is ours, then by all means let us have "daylight saving time." Anyone, however, may practice a sort of personal daylight saving plan by more prudent investment of an extra hour each day that might otherwise slip away unused.

"So teach us to number our days that we may get a heart of wisdom."

SAVING TIME

ORDINARILY WE THINK the best way to save time is to use some short cut, but this isn't always possible or entirely satisfactory. Sometimes short cuts result in a job poorly done or a project that must be started over. Then time is not saved but foolishly wasted. There is so much to do all the time that we are always interested in a more efficient method of getting more done in the time we have.

Paul, the Apostle, suggested a formula for saving time when he wrote to the Ephesians: "Redeem the time, for the days are evil."

The word "redeem" can be translated "save," although not as money is saved. We cannot pile up time, hoard it, and put it in safekeeping for future use. It isn't that kind of commodity.

The word "redeem" can be used to mean "save" in the sense that we can save from loss; we can repossess it; we can buy it back; we can reclaim it before it is gone, by using it to the best and fullest advantage.

To move a step farther, the word "time" can be translated to mean "opportunity." Thus, Paul, in effect, might have been saying "save your opportunities from loss, for the days are evil" or "make the most of your opportunities for the days are evil." If you get full value out of every minute, you are saving time in the best possible way.

When Paul said "the days are evil," he knew what he was talking about. Take a brief look at some of the events of his life: He was often at the point of death; five times he got forty lashes; three times he was beaten by the Romans; three times he was shipwrecked; he was stoned, many times he was starving; cold, and poorly clad. Certainly he didn't have a dull life. You could say that it was lacking in rewards. He didn't enjoy much prestige and he didn't accumulate any wealth. According to present-day standards, his life was a pitiful, shameful waste. But Paul, himself, didn't think so. He described his life as a constant pageant of triumph!

Paul had one all-consuming purpose in life. He took advantage of every opportunity, including all of these adverse situations, to accomplish it. He had a message that he considered so important that his personal reputation and welfare dimmed to insignificance by comparison.

Paul seemed actually pleased to be dragged before

the authorities, for it gave him a chance to tell them about Christ. He knew that Jesus Christ was the Son of God come in the flesh. There was no uncertainty or doubt in his mind and he didn't miss a single opportunity to "speak his piece."

His utter fearlessness bewildered his tormentors. They couldn't help wondering where he got his courage. He explained it this way, "I am not ashamed for I know whom I have believed, and am persuaded that He is able to keep that which I have committed unto Him against that day." His was an unshakable conviction that went far beyond mere intellectual acceptance. Thus he made the most of every opportunity. He redeemed the time.

This formula works and it can save time and souls too.

IF I FIND TIME

THERE IS A HANDY little triumvirate of tried and proven methods for avoiding getting involved in things. In spite of being obviously trite and overworked, we use them repeatedly as though they were fresh and original every time.

The first excuse is a little weak as it leaves a possible loophole. We say, "I'll do it, if I find time." This is a conditional promise to perform based upon the unlikely possibility that there might be a little portion of unused time lying around the house. If this should ever happen, then we are stuck with the job.

The second method, somewhat more definite, sounds a little peevish and tinged with self-pity. It implies we were short-changed when the daily allotment of twenty four hours was handed out. "I would do it, if I had more time." Of course, if we had not been unfairly discriminated against in the matter of time, this one would trap us.

The third, a point-blank, outright refusal leaves no room for argument. "I can't do it. I just don't have time." This one is best, for it leaves no doubt. No equivocation is possible.

Granted, most of us get involved too deeply sometimes and actually do find we are so busy with many things that the time we have, which is all the time in the world, really, just doesn't cover all the things we would like to do. While we have crammed each day to overflowing, a little careful self-examination may reveal that we are not honestly making the most of our time. There is no way to recapture it once it is lost or foolishly spent. The time that we use needs to be carefully invested in what has real importance or we won't have enough to go around.

With each year we get 8,760 hours. Ordinarily that will break down about as follows: 2,290 hours for sleep; 2,100 hours for work; 700 hours for eating and attending to personal needs. We will putter around and entertain ourselves about 600 hours. We will spend about 400 hours in improving our minds, reading. We should be in church worship services about 100 hours every year. That leaves us 2,000 unallocated hours.

How well we use the time we must devote to the duties of living, and how well we invest that extra 2,000 hours will determine how much we can afford to get "involved" in.

Sometime—when you have time, that is—figure it out for yourself!

TREADMILL

IN A RECENT ISSUE of a travel magazine there was an example of "water power" in Korea. Two sparsely clad peasants were pictured treading a revolving waterwheel, their scrawny brown arms draped over a rough board across the top of a crude framework. By a constant walking motion they were causing the wheel to revolve and push water into an irrigation ditch.

There are times when life seems a little like that. It falls into a kind of tiresome pattern, repeating itself with such regular monotony, that we begin to question the value of it. It seems to be only a monotonous, meaningless, but inescapable trudge toward extinction.

Day after day the cycle revolves: we get up, go to work, rush from one thing to another, somehow always just a little behind schedule. We seem never able to accomplish as much as we think we should as round and round we go in an almost breathless chase, one day following hard upon another.

If life is to be more than a meaningless march toward nothing, we ought to check up on ourselves to see if we are doing what God wants us to do.

We have a natural desire to increase our worth. We

want to become significant citizens with standing in the eyes of society. We want to acquire a fair share of this world's goods for what can be done with them. Jesus never condemned this tendency to rise and become great, but He did mark out a road to true greatness for us. And it doesn't exactly coincide with the path we would like to follow to achieve it.

We think that greatness as individuals comes in direct proportion to the power we can acquire through control of money and goods. Many work toward the acquisition of that kind of power at the price of all kinds of human injustice and when they have their hands on it they think they have become great.

Jesus said that the road to true greatness lies along the way of voluntary service. He said "Whoever would be first must be servant of all. Whoever would be greatest must be least of all."

Here is another example of the paradoxical kind of reasoning that makes the Christian philosophy of living difficult to accept. Our natural inclination is not to follow the way of sacrifice and service. Jesus' plan for a life that would have meaning and that would be something more than an endless, pointless treadmill, involves learning to love even those who persecute us. It means being willing to serve even those who are hardly worthy of service. It means being ready to forgive. It means turning the other cheek.

That kind of life can't be frustrating or monotonous. It has too many challenging opportunities that require real rugged individuals.

HURRY UP, YOU'LL BE LATE!

I SAW A CLEVER cartoon recently depicting a mob of people rushing, struggling, and shoving their way up a steep mountain side. As they reach the top, they just drop off into space. But the people who are feverishly trying to get to the top can't see that, so they keep battling their way up. However, there is one fellow making no attempt to join this rush to the top. One of the harassed pilgrims has stopped long enough to pull at his arm and is saying, "Hurry up, you'll be late!"

The day-by-day struggle for existence can be such an abortive experience if we do not know where we are going nor why.

To each of us has been given a life, certain talents, and certain opportunities. What we choose to do with them is an important decision. We can grub for an existence. We can take care of "number one" and let everyone else fight his own battle. We can go all the way through life under the whiplash of our desire to make money by whatever means. We can descend to the level of the brute whose progress through life is marked by violence and hatred. We can be indifferent, shiftless, and irresponsible, thinking the world owes us a living. We can pour all our interest and effort into flippant, meaningless things that are here today and gone tomorrow. Or we can, with determination, follow a plan and a pattern that has purpose and direction.

One of the most effective people we know was the Apostle Paul. He knew what he was going to do, where he was going, and what was really important. "This one thing I do . . ." he said, and in the power of the Holy Spirit (available to any one of us) he headed in that direction.

To make disciples of all nations is the most important thing that any of us has to do. There is tremendous urgency about the task. Christ said, "I must work the works of Him that sent me while it is called today for the night cometh when no man can work." It is an awesome but wonderful thought that God has given to man the important job of telling the world the message of salvation. He might have chosen another way. He might have sent legions of angels, but He told us to preach the Word in season and out of season. After two thousand years there are yet many places to which the Word of the Lord has not been carried. The field is certainly not over-crowded—it is wide open.

Before we plunge headlong after the on-rushing mob,

we would do well to question the direction and look into the end result of the foreward lunge.

When they pull us by the arm and cry, "Hurry up, you'll be late!" We might well inquire "Late for what?"

LEARN TO SAY "NO"

IN A WASHINGTON LABORATORY there is a large lens—three feet across. This lens gathers the sun's rays and focuses them on a spot several feet below. It is hot on that spot, so hot that they haven't been able accurately to measure the intensity of the heat because it melts the instruments used to measure it. Yet nothing has been added to the sun's rays to increase the temperature. It is just three feet of ordinary sunshine, focused and concentrated on one spot. When scattered, those rays are only mildly felt, but when concentrated into a single area they have the power to melt steel.

We are weak and ineffective when we try to spread ourselves too thin. We are like the poor fellow who was dubbed "Jack of all trades and master of none." He was a dabbler. He messed around a little with everything and never became much good at anything. To make the most of life's opportunities, we must learn to concentrate our efforts.

It requires judgment and discernment to discriminate between the many demands that are made on us. Some things we ought not to do because it will hinder our efforts in areas where we are more highly skilled and better qualified. Nor should we accept responsibility for tasks which we cannot bring successfully to conclusion when someone else stands ready, able and willing, to do the job. Learning to say "no" at the right time is one of life's most difficult problems. On the other hand, some of us succumb to an unwillingness or downright laziness which prompts us to say "no" to everything, without seriously examining our fitness or ability to perform. We cannot do everything, but we surely should do something. A Chinese philosopher said, "A man ought to decide what not to do in order to decide what he ought to do."

Every day presents a multitude of demands upon us and we must choose each day whom we will serve and what we will do. A starting point might be to check these demands against the basic criterion: Do they have eternal significance? Then we can establish priorities accordingly. Once having started a project we consider worthy, we ought to concentrate our efforts on it and follow through to the best of our ability.

ALL I DO IS WORK

I OFTEN FIND MYSELF starting one of my infrequent letters with the unoriginal excuse: "I've been so busy, it seems all I do is work. . . ."

We envy people who can be idle. We dream someday we will arrive at the state where we don't have to work if we don't feel like it. When the alarm rudely awakens us in the morning, we must fight the temptation to turn it off and go back to sleep. We would like to be free from the tedium of daily toil.

However, since the beginning of time it has been our lot to work. It says in Scripture, "There is nothing better than that a man should enjoy his work, for that is his lot."

Sometimes work has been referred to as a curse because when God drove Adam and Eve out of the Garden of Eden He told them, "Cursed is the ground because of you. In toil you shall eat of it all the days of your life and in the sweat of your face you shall eat bread." It is true that work became an integral part of that curse that sin brought down upon us, but work in itself is not a curse. In fact, if everything had gone as God planned it, we would all be "gardeners" or "gardener's helpers" for when God put Adam into the Garden, He instructed him to "dress and keep it." Woman was created to be Adam's helper.

Work, according to God's concept of it for us, is a creative activity—not a curse. It is the natural exercise of man to preserve and improve that which God has given. It is to be engaged in together with God. It is not the thing we do to live, but the thing we live to do.

The habit of thinking of work as something we do to make money is so ingrained in us that it is difficult to evaluate our work in terms of accomplishment. Our test for any task is more often, "What will it pay?" than, "What good will it do?"

Our concept of work is a little unclear because employers are obsessed with the notion that they must find cheap labor and the workers have the idea that they must get the best paying job. As a result, many find themselves in work that is neither productive nor satisfying. It is when work is looked on purely as a means to making money that it becomes a hateful task-master and we its slaves.

The contented worker, whatever he may be doing, who is interested in the net result of his work, and who takes pride in a job well done, isn't going to "chisel" on the time he puts into accomplishing it. The seventh commandment, "Thou shalt not steal," covers the frittering away of the employer's time too. It is no less a crime or a sin to take an unearned salary than it is to take cash from the till.

One cannot be proud of the results of work that is spiritually degrading, or that involves a series of financial trickeries, or that results only in the production of vulgar or useless trivialities. A job well done, a product of usefulness and real value is a source of genuine pride and a high type of satisfaction that is a richly rewarding compensation for the effort and time that has been expended upon it.

The Bible states that work is a gift which we ought to enjoy: "It is God's gift to man that every one should eat and drink and take pleasure in all his toil" (Ecc. 3:13).

We all tend to gripe a little sometimes, but in America no one takes that too seriously. If we know that our work is contributing to the world's welfare, we aren't really complaining when we say "All I do is work. . . ." We are just letting off steam. We are all human, and we get weary—even of well-doing, but if we live by the Spirit, we should also walk by the Spirit and as Paul told the Galatians: "Do not be deceived; God is not mocked, for whatever a man sows, that he will also reap. For he who sows to his own flesh will from the flesh reap corruption; but he who sows to the Spirit will from the Spirit reap eternal life . . . so then as we have opportunity, let us do good to all men, and especially to those who are of the household of faith."

WHERE IS THE SLOT?

PARKING MY CAR in a small town recently, I discovered a parking meter with which I was unfamiliar. When I wasn't able to find the slot for my coin, I became annoyed and muttered out loud, "Why don't they make these things standard so you'd know where to put the nickel!"

Then in desperation I read the instructions which were very clear. I was a little embarrassed to see that there was even an arrow pointing to the coin slot.

Many people become irritated and dissatisfied with life because they are stumbling around in the dark, groping for familiar objects to guide them, grasping for the nearest thing to keep from falling on their faces. I think sometimes God exerts pressure that will make us sufficiently disturbed so that we will, in desperation, if necessary, read His directions. He has spelled it all out for us in His Word. It's all there and clearly legible. If we will let Him, He will even point the arrow for us so that we may know just where to go.

A young woman who had answered the call to the mission field told a friend that she felt God had definitely called her into that type of Christian service.

Her friend said, "I don't think God has ever called me to do anything."

The young missionary replied, "But have you been within calling distance?"

We don't have to fumble around trying to find the slot in which we belong. God will show us, if we get close enough to Him to hear Him. When we know what He wants us to do and where He wants us to go, then we must get busy and prepare ourselves in the best way possible so that we may not be unprofitable servants.

Every Christian is a full-time servant of the Lord in whatever profession he is engaged. Secular work is sacred too. Some of us are called to a particular job as a true vocation as specifically and as unmistakably as others are called to some special form of service in the Church.

The Apostles were right when they complained that they didn't think they should leave their primary business of preaching the Word to serve tables. Likewise, one *who has been called* to serve tables need not feel that she must leave her profession in order to serve the Lord.

When you find the "slot" where God wants you, you can make it a Christian occupation, for a Christian person truly praises God by the very excellence of his work.

THE PRESENCE

IN THE LOBBY OF THE dormitory where I lived while in college there was a picture which I believe is called "The Presence." The painting depicts the interior of a beautiful cathedral. At first glance I was impressed with its elegance, and then I noticed the figure standing in the shadows. There, just inside the door of the church, stands Jesus. He appears reluctant to enter this glittering sanctuary.

Perhaps it was not at all the impression that the artist wanted to create, but the picture somehow gives me the sad feeling that Jesus, the Son of God who became a simple, poor, humble man, does not feel quite at home in this elaborate temple.

Once Jesus took three of His disciples to the top of a mountain where He became transfigured before them. Elijah and Moses appeared and spoke with Him. Then a voice was heard out of heaven saying, "This is my beloved Son with whom I am well pleased, listen to Him."

It must have been an electric moment that filled the disciples with conflicting emotions. Now they knew who Jesus was.

Then Peter, the impetuous one, had an idea. "Lord," he said, "it is well for us to be here—let us build three temples, one for you, one for Moses, and one for Elijah and let us remain here to worship you."

Peter was so intent upon his desire to worship Jesus that he did not sense the selfishness of his plan. He forgot entirely that there was a whole world full of people with a similar need for this knowledge of Christ and this worship experience. He didn't give a thought to any missionary responsibility. Momentarily he forgot the deep hunger of all the people who had longed, as he had, for the day of the Lord.

It is easy to become selfish in worship. It would be nice to be able to erect a beautiful temple and then relax in it without feeling the uneasy compulsion to go out into the highways and byways and compel others to come in. Without deliberate intention, a congregation that has justifiable pride in its building and a keen awareness of its own parish needs can become so engrossed in itself that it is blind to the "fields white unto harvest."

Who has not heard the well-intentioned but selfish suggestion: "Let's take care of our own needs first and then if there is anything left over. . . ." It is one of the many paradoxes of Christianity that the more we give away the more we receive for ourselves. Jesus, in the Sermon on the Mount, put it this way, "Give, and it will be given to you; good measure, pressed down, shaken together, running over, will be put into your lap. For the measure you give will be the measure you get back."

If the building of a beautiful church in any way hinders its missionary outreach, that temple is already defiled. It costs a great deal to build a church and the temptation is there to cut the mission budget "at least until the new church is built." To keep up both a full mission program and an aggressive building program means a heavy load on the members that requires sacrifice. But what do we have that we have not received? Can we not trust God with His own money to do His own work in full confidence that He will not forsake us in the process?

The church has the most important purpose and program in the world: the sending out of the truth and the light of Jesus Christ into the dark corners. It has the only answer to man's need in an age of defeatism. Spreading the Gospel is its only reason for existence. If we curtail that program, then why do we build a temple? Do we believe we are constructing an habitation for the Lord? Then we have not read carefully what Paul said to the men of Athens (Acts 17:24:28).

"The God who made the world and everything in it, being Lord of heaven and earth, does not live in shrines made by man, nor is he served by human hands, as though he needed anything, since he himself gives to all men life and breath and everything. And he made from one every nation of men to live on all the face of the earth, having determined allotted periods and the boundaries of their habitation, that they should seek God, in the hope that they might feel after him and find him. Yet he is not far from each one of us, for in him we live and move and have our being; as even some of your poets have said, 'For we are indeed his off-spring.' "

"Who is able to build him a house, since heaven, even highest heaven, cannot contain him?"

So great a God is willing to dwell within the very heart of the believer and He asks no better shrine there than a humble and contrite spirit provides.

BUILD TEMPLES INTERNAL

THE CONGREGATION WAS having its services in our half-finished new building since our old church which had been sold was already housing another smaller congregation. It was a real thrill to watch the progress from week to week and to see our dream gradually become reality. We knew our new church would seem even more wonderful to us when it was complete because we had worshipped God in the midst of the construction and every member was excited over the addition of each new brick.

Driving home from services, I was humming snatches of that strong, stirring anthem "Build Temples Eternal" which our choir had sung that morning. When I came to portions where I knew the words I would burst out in full song. I don't know if it was a slip of the tongue or a sudden flash of inspiration, but I found myself singing "Build Temples Internal" instead of "Eternal."

I suppose, after all, the construction of an internal temple is the building program of every individual Christian. Following the blueprint as we find it in the Bible and under the guidance and direction of the Master Builder, the Christian is gradually erecting a holy place for God, a temple still unfinished although already inhabited. Day by day more rooms are added, the altar is raised, and windows are put in for the light to come through. Every year should find it nearer perfection, although we know that this temple within will not really be complete or perfect until it becomes an eternal temple.

For many years during the second world war, material restrictions and the shortage of manpower made it impossible to build at all. But then plans came out of mothballs and all over the country full-scale building programs were begun, producing better facilities with which to serve an enlarged area in the Kingdom.

It is encouraging to see churches optimistically garnering funds, laying long-range plans, and building solidly for the future when scientists, economists, and politicians predict there will be no future—or at best, they foresee only a dim and uncertain future. While they proceed at full speed to produce for our defense the weapons which they fear may cause the disintegration of the whole world in a matter of minutes, the church calmly proceeds with plans for an expanded program of Christian education and an extended outreach in mission activity.

You see, the church knows that whatever men do to forestall or hasten the date of total annihilation which they are so sure is imminent, the church is bound to its task of acquainting the world with Jesus Christ as rapidly as possible. The church is under orders to get busy, to redeem the time for the days are evil. This is hardly the time to retreat or retrench. This is the time to go boldly forward and to build stronger and better than ever.

The church is not unaware of impending world conflict. The church has its eyes on eternity, and, as it proceeds with its program, it is helping people to build indomitable temples internal which cannot be destroyed by nuclear fission or any other weapon. Temples built for eternity within the very hearts of the people will never be touched by weapons which can destroy only the body.

Writing to the Corinthians, Paul several times refers to the Christians as the "temple of God." In I Cor. 3:16 he says, "Do you not know that you are God's temple and that God's spirit dwells in you?" He continues with the warning, "If anyone destroys God's temple, God will destroy him. For God's temple is holy and that temple you are."

While we were in the process of building our church, we found it necessary to hire a man to serve as watchman when the builders were not around the new building. It was his job to protect the property from vandalism and to keep thieves from appropriating our dearly bought materials, both those within the walls of the building and those which were stacked outside around the premises.

How easily vandals get into our internal temples! What has been carefully erected on Sunday at the worship service may be torn down and destroyed on Monday. The stained glass window through which the light of His Word filtered in at personal devotions, may be smashed to bits by one conversation that degenerates into gossip.

Unfortunately, the vandals that defile our internal temples are quite often not strangers to us. It is often we, ourselves, who destroy that which has been built in us. Jesus says, "Watch and pray that you do not enter into temptation." It takes full-time, constant vigil to protect that precious structure from destruction. We must set a watchman on duty lest we defile that house of God which is within us.

POTENTIAL LIGHT

ON THE TOP SHELF of a closet off the kitchen there is a supply of extra bulbs, all sizes—some big 100 watt bulbs, some 60 watt, some only 25 watt. Altogether they represent perhaps several thousand watts. In each of those individual bulbs are all the tiny wires which make it possible for them to transmit light.

But it is dark in that closet. It is just as dark as though there were no bulbs on the shelf at all. Because all those bulbs are only potential light.

Like those little bulbs, we have the latent possibility of transmitting light. Scripture is full of reference to the light that is in us, such as: "Once you were darkness but now you are light in the Lord."

Like those extra bulbs, if we are not connected to the power, the real source of the light, the world about us will be just as dark as though the spirit of God had never been planted in our hearts. We must be "plugged in" to the power line to produce an illumination.

One of the office boys came in to see me one day carrying what appeared to be an ordinary light bulb. Suddenly it lit up right in his hand. At first he tried to tell me that he possessed some unique power within himself that made the bulb burn; however, eventually he showed me how it was done. It was a trick bulb that had a tiny battery built right into the base. By touching the metal base to the ring on his finger, he made a contact which produced the light. Repeated demonstrations throughout the day of his wondrous "power" soon burned out the feeble battery.

Self-generated power just isn't enough to produce the light we have been instructed to send forth. We soon dim, and eventually burn out, if we depend on the power of our own personality, wit, charm, or intelligence. It takes a more dependable source to produce a steady, strong glow that won't be extinguished.

There are many different types and sizes of light, varying according to the use and the need for each. There are tiny little flashlights attached to key rings. They are intended merely to light up the key hole. There are huge beacons sweeping the sky. They guide planes and warn of danger. You don't need a beacon light to open the front door, nor would a tiny flashlight be much help to a speeding plane in the night. When each is used to full capacity as it was intended and draws power from a dependable source, it is serving a useful purpose.

We aren't all equipped with similar "wattage." Some of us are only little 10-watt spiritual lights, and it was never intended that we should illuminate wide areas.

Others of us have tremendous potential for sharing the light. If any of us have faulty wiring and a poor connection with the true source of light, however, we will only flicker weakly. If we are trying to generate our own power, we will soon burn out entirely. If we are only "potential light," idle on the shelf, the world will be no lighter because we are in it.

POWER STATIONS

SOME YEARS AGO I visited a power plant where a natural waterfall provides the force which turns giant turbines and motors to create and store electricity for distribution throughout a wide area around the plant. The guide showing us around the plant explained the process whereby waterpower is converted to electricity. We saw big signs all over warning of the danger of the high voltage. The guide explained that if the full force of the power which is generated there were turned loose into the homes and industries it supplies, it would burn them up. So, he explained, they have sub-stations at strategic points across the country where the power is cut down or boosted according to the needs of that particular area.

God has enough power to flood the whole world with a blinding, blazing light that could consume it in one flash. All His power is available to those who would do His work, but of course, we couldn't handle it in all of its full force either. So He must trim it down to fit our needs and transform it into units that we can use.

One of God's sub-stations where a particular type of power is available for a specific need, is in the wilderness experience of Jesus. There the power to overcome temptation was demonstrated. Anyone who would do the will of the Lord may draw on that power.

Another sub-station for power is in His experience in the Garden of Gethsemane. Here the human Jesus would gladly have given up the whole thing as He saw the horror that the coming days held for Him. But He found the power to endure when He threw the switch that turned His will into the will of God.

There is a very special power available at Golgotha, "the place of skulls." There Jesus, who had been subjected to all manner of human indignity, raised His voice clearly and resolutely to say, "Father, forgive them, for they know not what they do."

The grace to forgive, even in the midst of persecution, is the power that makes it possible to endure when taunts and terrors come upon us.

The greatest and most important source of power for the one who would shed abroad the light of Christ, is that which emanates from another garden where there is an empty tomb. If that tomb, which symbolizes power over death and promises resurrection power, were not empty, there would be no light for the world. It is mute evidence of the divinity of Jesus Christ. It authenticates His ministry and gives validity to His sacrifice. The empty tomb gives meaning to the Christian message.

Drawing on these sources where God's power is packaged to fit our needs, we can let our light so shine before men that they may see our good works and glorify the Father who is in heaven.

ACCOUNTABLE RESPONSIBILITY

Do you cringe a little when the word *stewardship* is mentioned? I do. Perhaps it is because the term has the connotation of money. Not that we have anything against money—in fact, most of us are rather fond of it—when it is headed in our direction!

It's just that the word *money* is almost a "dirty" word when it is implied that we ought to part with a little of it. We are jealous of our hard-earned cash. Most of us have little enough for our own use, without being constantly reminded that there are others who have less. We would like to ignore the fact that there are legitimate needs for which we have some personal responsibility.

The word *stewardship* didn't always refer to money. In fact, the word doesn't have a very pretty origin. Originally it was *sty warden*—keeper of the pigs. It was the name given to the man who was in charge of the pigsty. He was a hired man, a servant of the master, a man charged with responsibility for the care and feeding of pigs which belonged, not to him, but to the master of the household. He was expected to care for the pigs as carefully as though they were his own. Periodically the master would require an accounting. He was concerned that his property was being well cared for and that his investment in swine was profitable.

The word has undergone some changes over the years to become *steward* and the term *Stewardship* has developed from it to indicate *Accountable Responsibility* for that which is not our own, but over which we have been given supervision in trust with the right of use.

Obviously, when we consider the gifts of God which are manifold, we realize that our stewardship responsibility toward Him means accountabilty for considerably more than money. Money is only one of the gifts of God, only a symbol and a medium of exchange.

We ought not be irked when the word is mentioned. An accounting will be required of us, and those who refer to the subject occasionally are only helping us to remember that although we have nothing that we did not receive, we have accountable responsibility for all that we have.

"And if you have not been faithful in that which is another's, who will give you that which is your own?"

CANCELLED CHECKS

I STOPPED AT THE BANK one day to pick up my cancelled checks for the past month. Returning to the office, I thumbed through them, curious to know where my money had gone, figuring where I might have been more economical, and wondering where I had been unwise in my expenditures.

Punched full of holes, these checks no longer have value in themselves except as receipts, yet they paint a vivid picture of the individual whose signature made them valid. The food, clothing, rent, transportation, amusements, and charity for which I have spent money are all reflected in my cancelled checks. They give some indication of my needs, what I consider important, and where my extravagances are.

I thought as I looked through them: this is a picture of my life, but I would hate to believe that it is a complete picture. In fact, it is a rather distorted picture—something like the reflection in a trick mirror. There is a resemblance, but it is certainly not a true or complete image. This is an exposure only of my financial life. There are many other things that come in to enrich life and that flow out to enrich the lives of others. Over all of these things I have some control and a measure of responsibility too. These things, together with the money I have acquired, make a more nearly accurate picture of my life.

I wonder what God sees when He looks over the "cancelled checks" which represent the time we have spent, the opportunities we have squandered, and the talents we have used?

Have we channeled a fair portion of all those things back into the service of the Giver? We have an obligation. "For unto whomsoever much is given, of him shall much be required."

ALL THAT WE HAVE

WE STAND IN THE sanctuary on Sunday morning and sing:

"All that we have is Thine alone—a trust, O Lord, from Thee."

We feel all warm and smug because we have just dropped a dollar bill into the collection plate. This, we feel, has discharged our personal responsibility for going and making disciples of all nations.

We have already forgotten that on the way into church we refused to have devotions at an organization meeting. We were too busy to visit the Old People's Home. It was too cold, or too hot, or too wet to come to a Bible study meeting.

We sing in a loud, confident voice, "All that we have is Thine alone . . ." but we refuse our time, talent, sympathy, love, understanding, interest, and enthusiasm. There are a lot of important things in the Kingdom of God that need such gifts and such participation more than they need our money!

We have come a long way since the days when collections were noisy with nickels and dimes clattering into the plate on Sunday morning. But now we have acquired a new disease—dollaritis!

We just give a dollar here and a dollar there without considering the relative merits of the various appeals that come to us. Some of them aren't worth a dollar. Some of them need *us* more than they need our dollar. Some of them should require of us a great deal more than a dollar. It is easy, comparatively speaking, to depend on a crumpled piece of negotiable currency to fulfill our obligations.

"All that we have is Thine alone—up to one dollar, that is."

ACTIVE OR PASSIVE

PEOPLE DON'T OFTEN use mottos as part of their interior decoration schemes these days. This generation is too sophisticated to be moved by such sentimental stimuli, I suppose. My inclination, too, when I see a motto in someone's home or on a desk, has been to ignore the pithy little message. Recently, however, I saw one that made me think. It was a "covenant" type of thing, a sort of statement of intention. The sentence that caught my attention read in part:

"To yield my life to the living Christ and permit His life to be formed in me."

A noble aspiration, I thought, but could it be more than a good intention?

It seemed to me that it would not be easy to live up to such a lofty ideal, but as I thought about it, I wondered if the key to it doesn't perhaps lie in those two words "yield" and "permit."

They are passive words. They do not anticipate a great program of activity, but rather, they suggest flexibility and submission. Further, they imply a choice: to struggle or to relax, to direct or to be directed.

In the miracle of human creation when God breathed life into us, He gave us the freedom to make our own choices. We have the right to "yield" and "permit" but unfortunately, we also have the "right to do wrong." Those are active words—aggressive, defiant, independent words that can only get us into trouble.

To "yield" and "permit" makes it imperative that all blockades be removed which may impede the free flow of the power of Christ into daily living. This can be accomplished only when we lower our defenses, yield to Christ and permit things to happen.

Choosing to "yield" and "permit" in no way contradicts what we mean by the third article of our creed: "I believe that I cannot by my own reason or strength believe in Jesus Christ or come to Him, but the Holy Ghost has called me by the Gospel . . ." We cannot assist the Holy Spirit in His work, but we can choose to cease to resist and give Him free course.

Although "yielding" and "permitting" requires a certain passivity from us to begin with, when the living Christ dwells within, we become supercharged for activity. His influence reaches out with our hands, His love yearns over the needy with our hearts, His feet walk where we walk. He uses everything we are and everything we have to accomplish the ultimate purposes of God.

A yielded life makes right choices habitually because it is under the guidance of a heart of love, a mind of eternal wisdom, and a will to accomplish the higher good. When we have yielded our lives in this way, we live "good" lives, not because the law demands that we live that way, although obviously our manner of life will conform more closely to the law too. We live "good" lives not because custom or society dictates that we follow certain behavior patterns. We live "good" lives not because as Christians we ought to be different but because we are different. We live "good" lives because in "yielding" and "permitting" Him to shape our lives we are transformed from within by the "renewing of our hearts and minds."

ONE HUNDRED PERCENT INTEREST

I READ A BOOK recently in which the author devoted one whole chapter to bemoaning the great poverty of God. God is not poor. God is not dependent upon handouts from us!

God, the Almighty, the Creator, the Ruler of the universe, does not have to beg and cadge for a few shekels that His creatures deign to toss in His general direction.

It isn't reasonable that God needs, actually needs, the few paltry dollars we can spare for His work. He, to whom the cattle upon a thousand hills and all the silver and gold in the world belong; He, who can speak and bring life into being; He, who can feed thousands with a loaf of bread and a few fish, certainly doesn't depend on the pittance we dole out to Him.

We give not because God needs our gifts. God has planned His economy this way because He knows that we need to give. What God really needs is disciples—

faithful followers who hold back nothing that the Master may ask.

Stewardship is discipleship, and discipleship is total consecration of all that we have, so that the task which Jesus left for us to do might be done. Whatever it takes to make disciples of all nations, as He said we should do, that is what we must be willing to give. It may require our very lives.

Delineating the qualifications for discipleship one time, Jesus said, "So therefore, whoever of you does not renounce all that he has cannot be my disciple."

Discipleship, or total consecration, or stewardship, whichever you want to call it (it is all the same thing) requires relinquishing our hold on not just our money. It means being willing to give up anything that may be required.

It costs a lot. It costs trusting enough to risk everything on the strength of the promises of Jesus. But do you realize He has promised a one hundred percent return on our investment and a bonus of eternal life too?

Once when Peter was complaining just a little bit about all that he and the others had given up in order to be disciples, Peter said, "Lo, we have left all and followed you. . . ."

Jesus answered him, "Truly, I say to you, there is no one who has left house, brothers, sisters, mothers, fathers, children, or lands, for my sake and for the Gospel who will not receive a *hundredfold*—now in this time and in the age to come eternal life."

Where can you do better than that?

A FINAL WORD

IN THE "FOREWORD" to this book we stated the premise that while we are all human and subject to human limitations, there is no limit to our possibilities if we assume our rightful place as children of God, for then we have access to all His resources.

Now, having looked at many areas of daily living in that light, do you not agree that we are something more than human if we subjugate our tendency toward selfishness, trust in God for wisdom and leadership, and try to do His will in the spirit of love so perfectly exemplified by Jesus Christ?

So you're only human—but you are God's chosen vessel, made of clay but dignified by the sacrifice of the Son of God, selected for service of the King!

Appendix

Appendix

SUGGESTIONS FOR THE USE OF THIS BOOK

PERHAPS MOST WILL use this book for personal reading, a chapter or group of chapters at a time. Reference to the table of contents will provide guidance in finding material to fit a particular interest or need.

The reader will find self identification in the essays, for they deal, for the most part, with common everyday experiences that point up the fact that while we are all human with similar problems and limitations, we do have access to all the power and glory of God.

For group use, the suggestions that follow may be helpful.

It is recommended that the Revised Standard Version of the Bible be used for the supplemental Scripture proposed in connection with each chapter. For a fresh and interesting comparison and further illumination, the same portions of Scripture might be read from *Inspired Letters* by Frank Laubach or from the following books by J. B. Phillips which are translations into modern English:

The Gospels (Matthew, Mark, Luke, John)
The Young Church in Action (Acts of the Apostles)
Letters to Young Churches (The Epistles)

The Book of Revelation (The Revelation to John)

After reading the chapter aloud to the group, the leader should attempt to make a personal application of the subject matter. Related Scripture, as suggested, could be read by other members of the group. Allow opportunity for discussion and questions. The leader or someone else should lead in prayer. This little devotional period could then be closed by singing one of the suggested hymns or something else appropriate.

ANY HOLES IN YOUR HEAD?

Supplemental Scripture:

Gal. 5:22-26

I Cor. 13

When you pray:

Thank God for human personality, for inner resources of character, for the more pleasant aspects of disposition which makes us individuals distinct from each other, and most of all for the fact that He considers the human being, with all of its weaknesses, of such value that He gave His Son to die for it.

Ask God for the insight to recognize, the grace to confess, and the will to overcome the sins of the disposition which beset us.

In the Name of Jesus, who possessed all human characteristics and controlled them, who was human enough to understand and divine enough to forgive us.

Suggested Hymn:
O That the Lord Would Guide My Ways

STRAIGHT DOWN THE MIDDLE

Supplemental Scripture:
James 4:12
Matt. 7:1-5

When you pray:
Thank God for trusting you with His important work in spite of your reluctance and timidity and for picking you up when you fall.

Ask God to hold your tongue when you would criticize; to point the way when you should be busy; to stiffen your courage when you fear a difficult job.

In the Name of Jesus, who said "Judge not, that you be not judged."

Suggested Hymn:
O Master Let Me Walk With Thee

HOW COME?

Supplemental Scripture:

I Cor. 7:17-24

I Cor. 7:32-35

When you pray:

Thank God for the good things which are yours: family, friends, health, a job to do, and a place in the Kingdom.

Ask God to reveal His will for your life so unmistakably that you can accept it happily and turn your attention to making the best possible use of the gifts He has given for the enrichment of your life.

In the Name of Jesus, who walked alone in perfect peace and contentment because He knew and did the will of the Father.

Suggested Hymn:

My Jesus, As Thou Wilt!

NO REQUEST REFUSED

Supplemental Scripture:

Luke 6:27-36

When you pray:

Thank God for His Word which can be taken literally and can be lived exactly as it suggests.

Ask God for an unselfish spirit that withholds nothing that another may need or desire, and for full confidence that God will replace any need created in our lives by such generosity.

In the Name of Jesus, who gave His all for us.

Suggested Hymn:

God's Word Is Our Great Heritage

HE MADE NO ANSWER

Supplemental Scripture:

Matt: 27:11-14

When you pray:

Thank God for the calm and poise of Jesus under persecution, for the defeat of His enemies by the powerful weapon of silence, for the invincible truth against which there can be no threat.

Ask God for a similar constraint when evil forces would tempt us to strike out in anger.

In the Name of Jesus, whose self-possession can be ours if we live in the righteousness and truth of God.

Suggested Hymn:

In the Hour of Trial, Jesus Pray for Me

HOW BIG ARE YOU?

Supplemental Scripture:

Luke 12:25-31

When you pray:

Thank God for health and strength and healing when it is needed; for daily sustenance; for providing atmosphere in which we can live and breathe and thrive.

Ask God for an enlargement of our concerns beyond our physical bodies to the vast realm of the spirit.

In the Name of Jesus, who was the very embodiment of Faith, Hope, and Love.

Suggested Hymn:

I'm a Pilgrim, I'm a Stranger

SINGING IN THE CRACKS

Supplemental Scripture:

Phil. 3:8-16

When you pray:

Thank God for a sound mind that is healthy and normal; for the advances which have been made in curing mental illness; and for doctors and nurses who have dedicated their lives to the care of the victims of mental disorders.

Ask God to give you worthy objectives in life toward which to direct your efforts and thoughts so that you can develop a strong positive personality and a healthy outlook on life.

In the Name of Jesus, who said, "I am the Way . . . take up your cross and follow me."

Suggested Hymn:

Jesus Calls Us O'er the Tumult

ACT YOUR AGE

Supplemental Scripture:

Gal. 5:13-26
Phil. 2:1-11

When you pray:

Thank God for emotional growth and stability.

Ask God to root out any self-interest that may unbalance your sense of values and turn you into a social misfit.

In the Name of Jesus, with whom our old nature has been crucified.

Suggested Hymn:

Jesus Keep Me Near the Cross

LOST AND FOUND

Supplemental Scripture:

Luke 9:23-27

When you pray:

Thank God for a Savior who understands human nature in all of its weakness, temptation, and fallibility.

Ask God to accept your life and to absorb it into His service of humanity so that you may be a complete person in Christ.

In the Name of Jesus, who willingly became a servant of man to make men the sons of God according to their birthright.

Suggested Hymn:

Thy Life Was Given for Me

THINK

Supplemental Scripture:

Proverbs 23

When you pray:

Thank God for leaders of government and industry who see man as a creature of God and apply their personal Christian principles to the administration of their business.

Ask God to create in us clean hearts and clear minds that we may never become dominated by the tyranny of either men or machines.

In the Name of Jesus, in whose likeness we are formed.

Suggested Hymn:

I Think When I Read That Sweet Story of Old

FRAGMENTATION

Supplemental Scripture:

Mark 6:30-31

When you pray:

Thank God for the distraction of multiple responsibilities which wards off any possibility of boredom or dispair.

Ask God for an island of calm in the midst of daily life for contemplation upon His glory and wonder and for renewal of strength to continue with the duties which are ours to perform.

In the Name of Jesus, who said to the raging sea, "Peace, be still" and it obeyed!

Suggested Hymn:

Where Cross the Crowded Ways of Life

ON THESE THINGS

Supplemental Scripture:

Phil 4:8-9

When you pray:

Thank God for creative thoughts by which the arts and sciences develop for the progress of civilization.

Ask God to help you keep your thoughts pure and to use your mental powers for the production of worthwhile ideas for the greatest good toward humanity.

In the Name of Jesus, who was pure, holy, righteous, virtuous, and altogether praiseworthy in thought and word and deed.

Suggested Hymn:

Holy, Holy, Holy

BURIED TALENT

Supplemental Scripture:

Matt. 25:14-30

When you pray:

Thank God for the talents He has given you and for those yet undiscovered.

Ask God to show you how best to use the talents you

recognize and to reveal others you may not suspect are yours. Ask for courage to use them in doing His will.

In the Name of Jesus, who can bless the least talent to our use and to His glory.

Suggested Hymn:
Jesus, Master Whose I Am

PUBLIC OPINION

Supplemental Scripture:
Mark 14:66-72
Acts 2:1-47
Acts 4:13-20

When you pray:

Thank God that although we may be reluctant to acknowledge Him as Father, He still considers us His beloved children and is ready to forgive and receive us back into His family.

Ask God to give the assurance that the truth, however unpopular, will ultimately be victorious; and to give us fearlessness to be true to our convictions, however the scoffers may taunt us.

In the Name of Jesus, who was forsaken, betrayed,

and denied by His friends but never deserted by God; who was and is God.

Suggested Hymn:

If God Himself Be for Me

A WARM BOTTLE

Supplemental Scripture:

I Tim. 6:17-19

When you pray:

Thank God for daily food, clothing, shelter, air to breathe, sun to warm, and all things that sustain the body.

Ask God to help you believe that He will continue to protect that which He has created in His image and that He will supply all of your needs according to His riches in glory through Christ Jesus.

In the Name of Jesus, who said that man does not live by bread alone, but who also recognized the physical needs of His followers and blessed a meager supply of food to feed thousands.

Suggested Hymn:

Children of the Heavenly Father

104

GRIM REAPER

Supplemental Scripture:
I Thess. 4:13-18
II Cor. 5:1-10
Luke 12:4-7

When you pray:

Thank God for a normal sense of fear which insulates us against danger; for the comfort of His Word which assures us of eternal life; and for reserving a place for us in His presence.

Ask God to remove all uncertainty and to instill a real desire for reunion with Him so that we may look at death with anticipation of heaven instead of in fear of the unknown.

In the Name of Jesus, who rose from the dead and lives to welcome us when we come home.

Suggested Hymn:
In Heaven Above

A SURE CURE

Supplemental Scripture:
Phil. 4:11-13, 19

When you pray:

Thank God that although we are unworthy we are

not worthless and that God considers us of infinite value; that God's wisdom and not ours has determined what our natural endowments shall be; that we have nothing to fear if we trust in Him.

Ask God for assurance that no real harm can come to those whose destiny is in His care.

In the Name of Jesus, who is always standing by ready and willing to remove all baseless fear.

Suggested Hymn:

God Will Take Care of You

WHAT TIME IS IT?

Supplemental Scripture:

Psalm 90:1-12

When you pray:

Thank God that He expects us to live only one day at a time for that is all we have, all we can manage, and actually all we need.

Ask God to provide His grace in a measure sufficient for each day so that we may rejoice and be glad in it.

In the Name of Jesus, who said, "Do not be anxious about tomorrow."

Suggested Hymn:

Still, Still With Thee

SAVING TIME

Supplemental Scripture:

Eph. 5:15-17

When you pray:

Thank God that two thousand years of scientific and cultural advances has not changed the basic fact that Jesus Christ holds the answer to all real human need.

Ask God for recognizable opportunities to tell of your experience with the meaning of forgiveness through Jesus Christ's atonement for sin.

In the Name of Jesus Christ, the Son of God, who is the same yesterday, today, and forever.

Suggested Hymn:

Stand Up, Stand Up for Jesus

IF I FIND TIME

Supplemental Scripture:

II Peter 3:8-10

When you pray:

Thank God that we have enough of worth and value to contribute so that many demands continue to be made upon our time.

Ask God for discernment to see where our plain duty lies and how best to utilize time so that we do the really necessary things first.

In the Name of Jesus, who always put first things first and thereby made His three-year ministry so fruitful.

Suggested Hymn:

Savior, Like a Shepherd Lead Us

TREADMILL

Supplemental Scripture:

Col. 3:12-17

When you pray:

Thank God for all the people who do tedious, monotonous work to make life more pleasant for us; and for those who must work during the lonely hours of night or on holidays to supply our needs.

Ask God to add His blessing to work that must be done and to show us its significance in the total picture of life so we may find satisfaction and pleasure in it.

In the Name of Jesus, whose peace can rule in our hearts continually as we move from one task to another.

Suggested Hymn:

Dear Lord and Father of Mankind

HURRY UP, YOU'LL BE LATE!

Supplemental Scripture:

Matt. 28:16-20

When you pray:

Thank God that He has a plan and a pattern for every life and that He has provided clear-cut instructions in His Word.

Ask God to show you a glimpse of His purpose for your life so that you neither become discouraged and quit trying nor that you plunge blindly ahead to destruction.

In the Name of Jesus, who will go with us all the way.

Suggested Hymn:

Work for the Night Is Coming

LEARN TO SAY "NO"

Supplemental Scripture:

II Cor. 9:6-15

When you pray:

Thank God for the freedom of the individual to express his views openly, to cast his vote as he chooses, to worship God unmolested, and to live without fear of reprisals.

Ask God to hold His protecting hand over our nation and people and to quickly deliver those who live under tyranny and oppression.

In the Name of Jesus, who was the great champion of personal freedom.

Suggested Hymn:

Jesus, Rule My Thoughts and Guide Me

ALL I DO IS WORK

Supplemental Scripture:

II Thess. 3:6-13

When you pray:

Thank God for the vitality and vigor you need for each day's work and for a job to do in the preservation and betterment of that portion of the world which is your particular area of responsibility.

Ask God to forgive the laziness that causes shirking of duty and to give you vision to see what needs to be done and how it fits into the pattern of creativity.

In the name of Jesus, who knew the limitless resources of God and drew on them for courage and endurance.

Suggested Hymn:

In Jesus' Name Our Work Must All Be Done

WHERE IS THE SLOT?

Supplemental Scripture:

II Tim. 4:1-5

When you pray:

Thank God that there are many ways in which to serve Him and that He does not consider any one service as more important than another when all is consecrated to Him.

Ask God to show you clearly what He wants you to do, to close doors through which you should not go so that it will leave no doubt what avenue of service He has planned for you in the advancement of the Kingdom.

In the Name of Jesus, whose meat was to do the will of the Father.

Suggested Hymn:

Hark, the Voice of Jesus Calling

THE PRESENCE

Supplemental Scripture:

Matt. 17:1-8

When you pray:

Thank God for His Church where His Word is taught and preached; where believers may encourage one another to seek to know and do His will; where manpower and money are dedicated to carry the message of life into the rest of the world.

Ask God to bless His Church, its pastors, teachers, and all true believers that they may continue to guard the truth from violation and to propagate the faith to all generations.

In the Name of Jesus, the only name given under heaven by which man may be saved.

Suggested Hymn:

Lord Jesus Christ, Be Present Now

BUILD TEMPLES INTERNAL

Supplemental Scripture:

I Cor. 3:16-17

Acts 17:24-28

112

When you pray:

Thank God that He prefers the human heart to temples made by hand and that He can guide and direct us from the very core of our beings.

Ask God to cleanse and purify our hearts so that it will be a fit place for the Christ to come in and stay; ask Him to help us understand this mystery of the ever-present indwelling Savior.

In the Name of Jesus, who reminds us that eternal vigilance is necessary lest we become defiled.

Suggested Hymn:

On My Heart Imprint Thine Image

POTENTIAL LIGHT

Supplemental Scripture:

Eph. 5:7-14
I Peter 2:9-10
Phil. 2:14-16

When you pray:

Thank God for the light that He sends down upon us by way of the sun, moon, and stars, in which we can live and move and grow food for our bodies; for the light which comes by the Holy Spirit as His Word is opened to us by which we come alive spiritually as new creatures with the hope and assurance of eternal life.

Ask God to shine through us more and more brightly so that we may show the way to others yet in darkness and to keep us closely connected to the source of power so that we may not grow dim when light is so badly needed.

In the Name of Jesus, the Light of the World.

Suggested Hymn:

The Morning Star Upon Us Gleams

POWER STATIONS

Supplemental Scripture:

I John 2:5-10
I John 2:7-11

When you pray:

Thank God that He does not expect us to do His work without providing us with the power we need to do it.

Ask God to forgive us for the power we waste because we do not use it; to show us how to use His power; and to continue to provide that which we must have to do His will.

In the Name of Jesus, who has all the power of heaven and earth.

Suggested Hymn:

O Christ, Our True and Only Light

ACCOUNTABLE RESPONSIBILITY

Supplemental Scripture:

Heb. 13:15-16

When you pray:

Thank God for all His manifold gifts over which He has given us charge. Let us never take even the slightest thing for granted as though we had any right to expect His bounty.

Ask God to forgive the thoughtless ingratitude and selfishness that would hoard His gifts in fear of the possibility that He may fail to pour out His blessings upon us.

In the Name of Jesus, who is the supreme gift of God to men.

Suggested Hymn:

Jesus, Priceless Treasure

CANCELLED CHECKS

Supplemental Scripture:

Luke 12:22-24

When you pray:

Thank God that in His Word is a perfect mirror that shows us what we are and then at the same time shows us the perfection of Christ that indicates what we may be.

Ask God to give an eternal slant to our thinking and living so that we may see beyond the temporal needs of the body to the beauty of the spirit.

In the Name of Jesus, whose Kingdom is not of this world but who moves continually among us to keep us safe for the great day of reunion with Him.

Suggested Hymn:

Thy Life Was Given for Me

ALL THAT WE HAVE

Supplemental Scripture:

Luke 12:16-21

When you pray:

Thank God that all that we are and all that we have is ours by reason of His mercy and love.

Ask God to keep us ever mindful that every good and every perfect gift comes from above and we have no right to withhold anything that He may need or desire for Kingdom service or to aid His other children who may have wants.

In the Name of Jesus, for whose sake we are blessed continually with every good thing.

Suggested Hymn:

We Give Thee But Thine Own

ACTIVE OR PASSIVE

Supplemental Scripture:

Romans 6:12-14

When you pray:

Thank God for the freedom to make our own choices in life and for the human will which makes us godlike.

Ask God for wisdom to make right choices; to help us stand firm when sin and error beat on our defenses and to yield gladly when God and good would mold and shape us into the likeness of the Perfect One.

In the Name of Jesus, who said "Not my will but Thine be done" and He permitted God to win complete victory over the devil thereby.

Suggested Hymn:

Take My Life and Let It Be

ONE HUNDRED PERCENT INTEREST

Supplemental Scripture:

Mark 10:23-31

When you pray:

Thank God that He has made positive promises of eternal reward by which our hope and confidence is made sure.

Ask God for a place in His band of disciples and ask Him to use you and the gifts you bring so that the day may be hastened when the whole world will know that He is God and in Him is peace and joy and righteousness forever.

In the Name of Jesus, who invites us to follow Him and become fishers of men.

Suggested Hymn:

God Calling Yet